50 THINGS TO KNOW
BOOK SERIES
REVIEWS FROM READERS

I recently downloaded a couple of books from this series to read over the weekend thinking I would read just one or two. However, I so loved the books that I read all the six books I had downloaded in one go and ended up downloading a few more today. Written by different authors, the books offer practical advice on how you can perform or achieve certain goals in life, which in this case is how to have a better life.

The information is simple to digest and learn from, and is incredibly useful. There are also resources listed at the end of the book that you can use to get more information.

50 Things To Know To Have A Better Life: Self-Improvement Made Easy!

Author Dannii Cohen

This book is very helpful and provides simple tips on how to improve your everyday life. I found it to be useful in improving my overall attitude.

50 Things to Know For Your Mindfulness & Meditation Journey
Author Nina Edmondso

Quick read with 50 short and easy tips for what to think about before starting to homeschool.

50 Things to Know About Getting Started with Homeschool by
Author Amanda Walton

I really enjoyed the voice of the narrator, she speaks in a soothing tone. The book is a really great reminder of things we might have known we could do during stressful times, but forgot over the years.

Author HarmonyHawaii

---

50 Things to Know to Manage Your Stress: Relieve The Pressure and Return The Joy To Your Life

Author Diane Whitbeck

There is so much waste in our society today. Everyone should be forced to read this book. I know I am passing it on to my family.

50 Things to Know to Downsize Your Life: How To Downsize, Organize, And Get Back to Basics

Author Lisa Rusczyk Ed. D.

Great book to get you motivated and understand why you may be losing motivation. Great for that person who wants to start getting healthy, or just for you when you need motivation while having an established workout routine.

50 Things To Know To Stick With A Workout: Motivational Tips To Start The New You Today

Author Sarah Hughes

50 THINGS TO KNOW ABOUT WOMEN IN ISLAM

IN THE LIGHT OF QURAN AND HADITH

Farah Khan

Cover designed by: Ivana Stamenkovic
Cover Image: https://pixabay.com/photos/hijab-woman-islam-fashion-exotic-3598271/

CZYK Publishing Since 2011.

50 Things to Know
Visit our website at 50thingstoknow.com

Lock Haven, PA
All rights reserved.
ISBN: 9781091868984

50 THINGS TO KNOW ABOUT WOMEN IN ISLAM

BOOK DESCRIPTION

Do you want to know the status of women in Islam?

Do you think Islam discriminate among men and women?

Do you want to know the rights of the women that Islam gives them?

If you answered yes to any of these questions then this book is for you...

50 things to know about women in Islam by Farah Khan offers a approach to look into the Islamic perspective of women. Most books on (topic) gives a picture regarding status of woman but do not tell you all the details regarding women rights and responsibilities in Islamic perspective. This book discusses the topic with evidences from Quran and Hadith at one place.

In these pages you'll discover the true islamic values. This book will help you to understand the status of women that should be given to her in this world.

By the time you finish this book, you will know all about the women in Islamic world. So grab YOUR copy today. You'll be glad you did.

TABLE OF CONTENTS

DEDICATION

It is dedicated to my Grandfather.

INTRODUCTION

"Whoever does righteous acts,
whether male or female, while he is
a believer, verily, to him We will
give a good life, and We shall pay
them certainly a reward in
proportion to the best of what they
used to do"

(Quran 16:97)

Allah has created everyone men or women with equal rights. The one who is superior in front of Allah is the one who is righteous in his deeds. Prophet Muhammad (Peace Be Upon Him) also mentioned this point in his last Sermon that only Taqwa (bypiety) and good actions can make us superior in front of Allah as he said:

*"All mankind is from Adam and
Eve, an Arab has no superiority
over a non-Arab nor a non-Arab
has any superiority over an Arab;
also a white has no superiority over
black nor a black has any
superiority over white except taqwa
(bypiety) and good action."*

(Sahih Muslim)

We get number of evidences from many instances
in Quran and Hadith about the equality of each and
every Human being regardless of gender, color, age,
tribe etc. Islam believes in fulfilling due rights
towards everyone whether its neighbours, women,
men, children, parents, teachers, animals etc.

In this book I have tried my best to clear the
concept of women in Islam which is most of the time
negatively portrayed by the society. Women in Islam
are the ones who are independent in every sense and
are empowered ones in their own way, not the way
the society defines but in the way Allah has told them
to be. Islam protects the individual status of women in
every possible way and has made sure that women do
not suffer in case of any hardships they face.

1.ROLE OF A WOMEN BY NATURE.

Allah has made this universe and has created everything in it with a purpose. The nature of every creature is according to the purpose for which that creature is born to fulfill. Every human passes through different phases of life and in every phase he/she has different responsibilities towards others. If we look at men, we can identify I must say different faces i.e father, brother, husband or son. Similarly Women also have different roles (faces) to play in her life she can be a mother, daughter, sister or wife. Islam has clearly defined responsibilities of these roles and whoever fulfills these responsibilities is surely the best amongst us.

Men and Women complement each other, for the society they act as two pillars upon which the whole society is built. They can take each others responsibilities if required but its not possible to replace men with women and vice versa.

If we talk about "women being independent" we always talk in terms of comparing her with men. While Islam does not compare man with woman but rather treats her as a human being who have her own individual traits and nature which in no way can be compared with any other creature on this earth.

2.WOMEN AS A SCHOOL FOR HUMANITY

Islam recognizes women as a whole school for humanity. When the baby comes to life, from the very first day he learns everything from his mother. Woman as a mother has great responsibility to build the respectable society. Social values are learned at home and are taught by mothers. The sense of love, honesty , truth, peace, trust etc all are learned through the type of values we have at our homes. Like school prepares us for our career, similarly mothers play a very important role in giving us a perspective for life, she is the school who teaches us how to stand strong for the life ahead.

3. EDUCATION OF WOMAN IN ISLAM

Education is very important for every man and woman. Education lets our minds open and lets us to understand this universe. Islam is the religion which came in the era when people were far away from education and were blindly following the old schools of thoughts. Islam stressed on the acquisition of knowledge without any segregation of gender. Prophet Muhammad (Peace Be Upon Him) said:
"The seeking of knowledge is obligatory for every Muslim" (Al-Tirmidhi, Hadith 74)

When we talk about women, Islam emphasis on their education as they are the building stones of any society. We can not build a well educated and sophisticated society if we don't have educated mothers.

Moreover we find many examples of Muslim women who are the famous scientists and scholars. Let me quote here an example of Hazrat Ayesha who was the youngest wife of Prophet (PBUH). Hazrat Ayesha was a Muslim scholar and is well known for teaching many famous scholars. She had a very good memory and is the narrator of most of the Hadiths. Hazrat Ayesha is not only famous for her knowledge but also for her active participation in social and political activities.

If we talk about the Pre-Islamic time the education was thought to be as a luxury for woman and it was very rare to give education to the girls. But Al-Shifa bint Abdullah was very intelligent and skilled in giving medical treatments even in that era. Hazrat Muhammad (P.B.U.H) asked her to teach his wife Hazrat Hafsah bint Umar about the treatment of the skin illness. This shows that how Islam encourages the seeking of knowledge for woman.

4. WOMAN AND HIJAB

Let me ask you here:
" What does Hijab means?"
Hijab means "to cover".
Now just think here for a moment
"What are the things that you might want to cover or hide from others?"
Most probably the things that are precious to us or the things that we want to hide as we fear others might do some harm to them.

For example, let me talk about the present world we youngsters are very fond of cellphones. when we purchase a brand new and expensive android phone the first thing we want to do is to have the protector so that we can prevent its screen from damage.

Why we do this?

We do this because cellphones are very precious and delicate.

So the answer lies here, Hijab is not for the society its not for anyone else rather it's the cover or protection for one's own self. So women must cover themselves in order to protect themselves from the harsh realities of the society.

Hijab does not suppress the women nor hold them back but rather it gives them power to get out in this cruel world and just focus on the things she wants to do. In the current liberal world most of the people have biased opinions regarding hijab but let us think here for a moment is it right to create an opinion regarding anyone based on their dress?

5. WHY MUSLIM WOMEN PREFER HIJAB.

The modern world talks about the independence and empowerment of Woman. On the other hand they have objectified woman only as a glamorous commodity who most of the time is used to seduce society for selling a product or attracting the clients for business. Woman has been thought of only entertaining the male dominant society by lesser clothes.

But how can anyone get independent or empowered by not covering themselves up. And why wearing hijab and no hijab is a matter of concern for anyone. The sole purpose of Hijab is to protect woman and keep people with evil intentions away from her. Hijab helps the woman to create her own identity purely through her work, skills, knowledge and wisdom rather than material grounds like beauty, skin and body etc.

*"O Prophet! Tell your wives and
your daughters and the women of
the believers to draw their
cloaks(viel) over their bodies(when
outdoors). That is most convenient
that they could be known as
such(i.e. decent and chaste) and not
molested."*

(Quran 33:59)

6. CRITERIA OF HIJAB

Now for the people who talk about inequality in Islam on the basis of Hijab, should know that revealing clothes are not allowed for Muslim man and woman both. There is a guidance about how to dress for both men and women in Islam, Moreover Islam asks men to observe modesty,

*"Say to the believing men that
they restrain their eyes and guard
their private parts. That is purer for
them. Surely, Allah is well aware of
what they do."*

(Quran 24:31)

a.   Women should cover their full body except the face and hands upto the wrist. If they want to cover them as well they can but its not obligatory.

b.   The clothes should be loose and should not reveal the figure.

c.   The clothes must not be revealing.

d.   The clothes worn should not be very bold and appealing that they attract the opposite gender.

e.   The clothes worn should not resemble the clothes of opposite gender.

f.   The clothes must not symbolize any other religion.

7. WORKING WOMEN IN ISLAM

In Islam woman are allowed to work outside of their home if it's necessary for her to meet her needs. Woman are allowed to work keeping in view the requirements of her hijab as Islam wants to ensure the protection and respect of its believing woman first. There are examples in Islam where woman worked with compassion and proved themselves.

One of the famous example is of Hazrat Khadijah al-Kubra who was the first wife of Hazrat Muhammad (P.B.U.H) was one of the famous business woman in her times. She used to hire trustworthy, honest and devoted managers who used to travel for her far away to carry out the business on her behalf. Hazrat Khadijah used to carry out the business with dignity, modesty and never

11

compromised her integrity in order to succeed in this male dominated world.

8. EXAMPLE OF WORKING WOMEN

There are many great examples of women from the Islamic history in participating actively in economic activities. Let me quote example of Al-Shifa bint Abdullah who was known for her intelligence and knowledge. She got education in the times when seeking knowledge was thought as a luxury for woman, She was expert in giving certain medical treatments and that is what her name represents. When Al-Shifa embraced Islam she asked Prophet (P.B.U.H) for continuation of her services and Prophet(P.B.U.H) allowed her to do so.

When Madina developed Hazrat Umar felt that there was a need for a market supervisor in order to control the market activities according to the teachings of Islam. Al-Shifa was then appointed as the market supervisor because of her vast knowledge and skills. After sometime when market spread even further another woman Samra bint Nahik was appointed as a market controller as It is reported by ibn Abd al-Barr, "She knew the Messenger of Allah, peace and blessings be upon him, during her lifetime. She would patrol the markets by enjoining good and forbidding evil. She would discipline people with a whip she had with her."

9. WOMAN AS BREADWINNER FOR FAMILY

In Islam men are thought to be the head of family and so they certainly have responsibilities to support their family. But where it gets necessary for women to support her husband or family in certain cases, she surely can according to her will as its not obligatory.

Let me quote one example here from the time of our Holy Prophet (P.B.U.H). Zainab bint Abu Mu'awiyah was married to Abdullah Ibn Masood who was a great example of dignity. Zainab was very skilled in making beautiful handicrafts which she used to sell in the market. Zainab made enough through her sales while her husband was the man of limited means.

She once heard Prophet (P.B.U.H) telling women to donate to charity even anyone has to sell her jewellery. She came back and asked her husband to inquire from Prophet(P.B.U.H) that whether she can donate to her husband as he does not have enough means, otherwise she will donate to someone else. Abdullah Ibn Masood asked her to inquire this herself as it would be better for clarification of the matter.

Zainab and another woman from the Ansaar went to inquire this matter and put their point of concern through Hazrat Bilal in front of Prophet (P.B.U.H). Upon which Hazrat Muhammad (P.B.U.H) replied that," They will have double reward for this: one for their kindness to relatives and other for zakat" (related by Al Bukhari)

This means that woman can help her husband this way in supporting the family and get rewarded while if man does the same then it will be his obligation and will not be considered as zakat. This means that in Islam the relatives or members of the family whom we are required to support like children, wife, parents and grandparents are not eligible for zakat while husband for wife stands eligible for zakat as she is not obliged to support him.

10. RIGHT OF MARRIAGE

Islam gives woman right to marriage according to her own willingness. Woman have full authority to choose her life partner with the consensus of her elders and this decision should be made keeping in view the Islamic values that we have. In Islam celibacy is prohibited, there is a Hadith,

> " When a man marries he has fulfilled half of his religion, so let him fear Allah regarding the other half ."

(Al-Tirmidhi)

This hadith clearly explains us the importance of marriage in our religion. Islam does not believes in having any kind of relation between men and women who are strangers to each other or are Na-Mehram. These type of relations are strictly prohibited because they lead to destruction of society on moral and social grounds. Islam supports the family system in which everyone fulfills each others rights. Islam has detailed instructions about how to fulfill rights of children, parents, husband or wife. For a Muslim male or female family responsibilities have priority over any other duty of this world.

11. CONSENT OF WOMEN FOR MARRIAGE

Islam prohibits any marriage where consent of bride is not taken. If woman does not like someone she is free to follow her heart and not get married to that person. In Sahih Al-Bukhari there is a hadith quoted by Abu Huraira,

"No female whether a widow or divorcee will be forced to marry anyone unless her express and categorical consent has been freely taken and in the same way a woman not previously married can never be forced to marry anyone unless her free consent and permission is taken."
(Sahih Al Bukhari)
Nikkah is the religious contract between man and woman and if any party is forced to enter this contract the contract is considered void as it is so for any other contract.

*"If parents force their daughter
to get married to someone against
her willingness then the marriage is
void"*

(Sahih Al-Bukhari)

So in Islam there is no concept of forceful marriage. Marriage is a beautiful beginning of new life for two people so willingness of both is very important for its success.

12. NIKKAH

In Islam the contract of marriage is called Nikkah. At the time of Nikkah both man and woman are asked for their consent. Consent is taken and Nikkah is done in front of witnesses (2 from woman side and 2 from man side) and a legal guardian of a woman. Nikkah must not be a secret matter it must be announced formally. For Nikkah woman should not be in Iddah due to the loss of her previous husband as a result of death or divorce.

13. RIGHT OF MEHR

Mehr is one of the conditions for Nikkah. Mehr is the asset or amount of money that is agreed upon by both sides. it is mandatory for groom to pay mehr to bride at the time of marriage after which bride becomes its sole owner. Mehr is given by the husband to his wife at the time of marriage and no one has any right over it.

Allah says in Holy Quran,

"And give unto the women, (whom ye marry) free gift of their marriage portions..."

(Quran, An-Nisa: 4)

The purpose of Mehr can be seen as the protection of woman and her rights, it can be seen as a token of commitment from man towards his wife. The amount that is promised as mehr is considered as a debt on man until it is paid by him. In case of his death the first thing to be paid is his mehr to wife before the distribution of his property as a result of inheritance.

The wife can free her husband from the obligation of mehr if she wants to do so, but she should not be forced or asked by anyone to do so forcefully.

14. DIVORCE

First of all divorce is not liked by Allah as it is quoted by Messenger of Allah (P.B.U.H),

*" The most hated of permissible
things to Allah is Divorce. "*

(Sunan Ibn Majah)

But Islam does give right to woman and man to get separated if they have no other better option. In our religion it is more easy for woman to get divorce as compared to man as there is no obligation for woman in such cases. Woman does not have to divide and share anything in case of separation whatever has been given to woman can not be taken back from her. This is for the security of her rights as man can not take advantage of women's property and wealth by the means of marriage.

While man has to divide his property in case of divorce if it was promised at the time of marriage. Moreover if woman requires support and maintenance from her previous husband then its a duty of man to provide that as well.

15. IDDAH AFTER DIVORCE

In case of divorce there is a waiting period of three months for women which is known as Iddah. This period is considered because if the woman is pregnant then the identity of the child can be accurately determined. Moreover man and woman can also try for reconciliation during this period.

It is mentioned in Quran,

"Divorced women remain in waiting for three periods, and it is not lawful for them to conceal what Allah has created in their wombs if they believe in Allah and the Last Day. And their husbands have more right to take them back in this [period] if they want reconciliation. And due to the wives is similar to what is expected of them, according to what is reasonable. But the men have a degree over them [in responsibility and authority]. And Allah is Exalted in Might and Wise."

(Quran 2:228)

16. RIGHT TO REMARRY

In case a woman is a divorcee or a widow and has completed her waiting period (Iddah) as required in both cases she is allowed to get married again to a person of her choice. Islam gives her right to get married again and there is nothing wrong with it. In this modern society most of the people do not follow Islam properly and does not approve of woman getting married again. But Islam gives woman a right to marry again if she wants. We get many examples from the sunnah of Hazrat Muhammad (P.B.U.H) that its considered as an act of kindness to offer support to a widow or divorcee through marriage. Most of the wives of Prophet (P.B.U.H) were widow before they married him.

17. RIGHTS OF A WIDOW.

Widow is a woman who is separated from her husband due to his death. Because of this loss she has to suffer emotionally, psychologically and financially. After the death of husband who is the supporter and head of the family, a widow is left alone with her children to support them. She has to face new challenges in upbringing of her kids and taking the matters of life to a next step alone.

18. IDDAH PERIOD FOR WIDOW

Keeping in view the nature of human Islam allows a widow to marry again in order to take care of her chastity and find emotional and psychological support. A widow can marry again after a certain waiting period which is called Iddah. The Iddah period for widow is four months and 10 days. It is stated in Quran ,

"And those of you who die and leave wives behind them, they(the wives) shall wait(as regards their marriage) for four months and ten days, and when they have fulfilled their term"

(Quran 2.234)

In case the woman is pregnant then she has to wait until baby is born as it is mentioned in Quran,

"And for those who are pregnant (whether they are divorced or their husbands are dead), their Iddah (prescribed period) is until they lay down their burden."

(Quran 65:4)

After Iddah she can find a husband who is kind towards her and her children. If she does not want to marry again because of her kids she will be given a great reward for this sacrifice.

19. RIGHT OF INHERITANCE FOR WIDOW

After the death of her husband the widow gets the right of inheritance from her husband's property. She is entitled to inherit one fourth if there are no children but in case where there are children she is entitled to eighth of what her husband leaves. It is also mention in Holy book Quran,

"And for wives is one fourth if you leave no child. But if you leave a child then for them is eighth of what you leave."

(Quran 4.12)

20. WIDOW & SOCIAL SUPPORT

Besides inheritance the first right of a widow and her children is to have a shelter which should be provided to her in case her husband has not left a house. In cases where a widow does not have enough inheritance and is unable to support her family then it is encouraged for society to support her through zakat and charity. The Holy Prophet (P.B.U.H) said as quoted in Sahih Al-Bukhari ,

"The one who looks after and works for a widow and for a poor person, is like a warrior fighting for Allah's cause or like a person who fasts during the day and prays all the night."

(Sahih Al Bukhari)

21.EXPECTATIONS FROM MARRIAGE

Holy Quran says,

"And they (women) have rights over their husbands as regard living expenses, etc.) similar (to those of their husbands) over them (as regards obedience and respect, etc.) to what is reasonable, but men have a degree (of responsibility) over them."

(Quran 2.228)

The husbands are responsible for bearing all the expenses of the women and children while women in return should respect and remain obedient to their husbands. But in cases where husband commands his wife to do things that are against humanity or orders of Allah and Prophet (P.B.U.H) she is not obliged to follow him.

22. GUARDIAN OF HOUSE

Muslim woman are required to maintain good behavior with their husbands. A good wife should obey her husband and protect her chastity, house, assets, children and other possessions of her husband in his absence. The last Prophet (P.B.U.H) said as mentioned in Sahih Al-Bukhari,

"The wife is the guardian of the house of her husband and his children."

(Al-Bukhari)

It is also stated in Quran,

"...So righteous women are devoutly obedient, guarding in [the husband's] absence what Allah would have them guard..."

(Quran, 4:34)

23. IMPORTANCE OF MAINTAINING GOOD RELATIONS WITH HUSBAND

It is clear that in Islam woman is responsible for upbringing of children and maintaining the house. while husbands are responsible for the outside matters. The woman are required to create the environment of kindness in her home, She should show affection towards her husband and provide him with love that is necessary for meeting his needs.

Allah has offered a great reward for a woman who maintains good relations with her husband and try to fulfill all his rights as required by our religion.Hazrat Muhammad (P.B.U.H) said,

"If a woman prays her five daily prayers, fasts her Ramadan, guards her chastity and obeys her husband, she may enter by any of the gates of the Paradise she wishes."

(Al-Tirmidhi)

24. RESPONSIBILITY OF HUSBAND TOWARDS WIFE

If Allah has made it obligatory for woman to obey her husband, then how can he forget and leave woman behind. Allah has given rights to woman which no other religion has ever given. First of all after marriage the full responsibility of what a wife desires and how to fulfill them is upon her husband keeping in view that they are within the boundaries of Islam. Husbands are responsible for providing food, shelter, clothes and other necessities of life to their wives. A woman however can spend the money that she earned where ever she wants without the permission of her husband or even telling him.

25. RELATION OF MARRIED WOMAN WITH HER PARENTS.

Islam does not allow husbands to stop women from meeting their parents or close family members and confining them to the house for no reason. It is not allowed in Islam for woman to change her name after marriage. In Islam every one is called by the names of their legitimate father and no one else, as told by Prophet (P.B.U.H),

*"Whoever calls himself by other
than his father's name (or
attributes himself to someone other
than his father), will be cursed by
Allah, the Angels and all the
people."*

(Ibn Maajah)

26. RESPECT OF WOMEN AS WIFE

Islam encourages husband to be kind towards his wife and there is a reward for the one who treats his wife well. Hazrat Muhammad (P.B.U.H) said,

*" The best of you is he who is
best to his wife."*

(Ibn Maajah)

Our Last Prophet (P.B.U.H) taught us through his actions that how well one should treat his wife. It is encouraged to praise ones wife in front of her and others. Muslim men should make life easy for their wives and they are told to participate in chores of the house and upbringing of children.

*Al-Aswad asked Aishah about
what the Prophet used to do at
home. She replied. "He used to
serve his household but when it was
time for the prayer, he would get up
for prayer."*

(Al-Bukhari)

Respect is the right of every woman and it is a
duty of husband to give her respect and guide her to
the right path whenever she is wrong rather than
insulting her and making her feel bad. Prophet
(P.B.U.H) told us,

*" No believer should be angry
towards his wife. If some of her
qualities are displeasing, there will
be many other qualities worth
appreciation."*

(Muslim)

27. CONDITION OF 4 MARRIAGES

Islam has allowed men that they can keep 4 wives but in cases where husband can give them equal rights. If husband does not have power to treat all the wives equally then he should not marry more than onces. Allah says,

"Marry women of your choice, two or three, or four; but if you fear that you shall not be able to deal justly (with them), then only one or (the slaves) that your right hands possess. That is nearer to prevent you from doing injustice."

(Quran 4:3)

Our Last Prophet (P.B.U.H) warned by saying,

" if a man has two wives and does not treat them equally, he would be raised on the Day of Judgment with half his body paralyzed."

(Tirmidhi)

28. KEEPING THE SECRETS OF SPOUSE

As women are required the to keep the secrets of their husbands and not to disclose their personal matters outside the house similarly men are also not allowed to disclose secrets of their wives. Allah's Messenger (P.B.U.H) said,

"The most wicked among the people in the eye of Allah on the Day of judgment is the men who goes to his wife and she comes to him, and then he divulges her secret."

(Sahih Muslim)

29. EXPRESSING THE LOVE FOR WIFE

In eastern societies most of the people don't bother to express their love openly for their wives as they fear that they will be made fun of doing so. While Hazrat Muhammad (P.B.U.H) showed us through his actions that there is no harm in expressing your love for your wife. This expression makes the relation strong and long lasting. It is important to to express yourself in order to keep your relation alive.

> *"Once Anas (may Allah be pleased with him) narrated that the Prophet (peace and blessings be upon him) was asked, 'O Messenger of Allah, which of the people is most beloved to you?'*
> *He answered: "`A'ishah."*
> *He was asked, 'And among men?'*
> *He said: 'Her father.'"*

(Ibn Majah)

30. IMPORTANCE OF SHOWING LOVE THROUGH ACTIONS

I don't think so that anyone would disagree with me saying that words have no importance if you don't consider them in your actions. Our actions may make someone feel loved even if we don't express them. While on the other hand if we don't prove through our actions our words will lose importance with the passage of time. We get many examples through sunnah of Prophet regarding the importance of expressing love through actions.

> *"Aishah (may Allah be pleased with her) reported that the Messenger of Allah would give her a vessel to drink, when she was menstruating, then he would look for the spot where she had put her lips on and put his lips on the same spot."*

(An-Nasa'i)

In another example we get the idea that how should we respect our wives and make others to respect them.

> *"Anas narrated that the Prophet had a Persian neighbor who was good in cooking soup. One day he prepared some soup and invited the Prophet to it. Aishah was present so the Prophet suggested to the neighbor that she should join them. The neighbor refused to include her*

in the invitation. The Prophet,
therefore, declined the invitation.
The Persian repeated the
exclusive invitation for the Prophet
who, once again, declined the
invitation.
In the third attempt, the Persian
neighbor invited both the Prophet
and his wife, Aishah (may Allah be
pleased with her). Then, the
Prophet accepted his invitation and
went with `A'ishah to the man's
house."

(Muslim)

Hazrat Muhammad (P.B.U.H) used to enjoy with wives through small gestures which made them happy and every action that Muhammad (P.B.U.H) did is a lesson for muslims. There is a one famous story of Hazrat Muhammad (P.B.U.H) and Hazrat Aishah narrated at many places.

Aishah reported that she
accompanied the Prophet in a
travel when she was still slim. The
Prophet told people to move
forward and then he asked `A'ishah

33

*to race with him. They had a race
and Aishah won.*

*In a later travel, when Aishah
had forgotten the race and had
already gained weight, the Prophet
told her to race with him again. She
declined, "How can I race with you
while I am in such a condition?"
The Prophet insisted and they did
have a race. The Prophet won this
time. He laughed then and said,
"Now, we are even."*

(Authenticated by Al-Albani)

31. STATUS OF DAUGHTERS

Daughters have a special status in Islam. Before Islam and even in this modern era some people consider birth of daughter as a burden but in Islam Allah has declared daughter as a blessing. As far as the concern is with the rights of daughter, Islam gives similar rights to daughter as to son and there is no discrimination upon them. Same type of upbringing and teachings must be given to both.

*"Ibn Abbas reported: The
Messenger of Allah, peace and
blessings be upon him, said,
"Whoever has a daughter and he
does not bury her alive, nor
humiliate her, nor prefer his sons
over her, then he will enter
Paradise because of her."*

(Sunan Abi Dawud)

Such great reward for upbringing of daughters what else other than Jannah Muslims want! This hadith clearly tells us about how important it is to educate a girl/daughter and taking care of her is. At one more place Hazrat Muhammad (P.B.U.H) told us,

"He who raises two daughters until their puberty will be with me in paradise like this (and he symbolized the proximity by showing two of his fingers with a slight gap between them."

(Muslim)

The respect that Islam gives to woman is hard to find anywhere else. Hazrat Muhammad (P.B.U.H) mentioned this in one hadith,

"If someone has three daughters and is patient with them and clothes them from his wealth, they will be a shield against fire for him."

32. RIGHT OF INHERITANCE (DAUGHTERS)

It is the primary responsibility of parents and brothers to educate daughters and prepare them for the life ahead. They should provide for them until and unless they get married. As discussed before daughter and sisters do have the right of inheritance. She gets half of her brothers share from her father's property. Allah has ordered us to do so in Quran,

"From what is left by parents and those nearest related there is a share for men and a share for women, whether the property be small or large,— a determinate share."

(Quran 4.7)

Quran regarding the portion of this share says,"

"Allah (thus) directs you as regards your children's (inheritance): to the male, a portion equal to that of two females: if only daughters, two or more, their share

*is two-thirds of the inheritance; if
only one, her share is a half."*

(Quran 4.11)

The reason to give more share to men as compared to women is basically due to the economic and financial responsibility that men carry according to the instructions in Islam, while women are free from any such responsibility.

33. DAUGHTER AND FATHER LOVE

Daughter and father have a very unique relation of love and respect. The first man that a daughter loves when she comes to life is her father. The strong the bond is the stronger the personality of a daughter will be.

We find number of examples from Prophet (P.B.U.H) life regarding father and daughter love and respect. Hazrat Aisha Bint Talha quoted Hazrat Aisha saying,

*"I have not seen anyone more
similar to the Messenger in speech
and dialogue than Fatima.
Whenever she entered the house, he
would greet her, kiss her hands and
ask her to sit near him. Likewise,*

37

when he entered the house, she
would greet him, kiss his hands and
etc......"

34. WOMAN AS A MOTHER

Parents are very important part of our lives, we come to this world and survive because of our parents sacrifices that they do for us without demanding any return. According to Islamic teachings we are ought to give respect, care, love and a high status in our lives to our parents. Prophet Muhammad (P.B.U.H) said,

" The one who pleases his
parents has pleased Allah and the
one who has angered his parents
has angered Allah."

(Kanz Al Ummal)

Among the parents we see that Islam regards mother with the slight higher status as compared to father due to the hardships she has to face in order to bring us to this life.

35. LOVE AND RESPECT FOR MOTHERS

Our last Prophet (P.B.U.H) said,

" Your heaven lies under the feet
of your mother."

(Sunan an Nasai)

This means if we treat our mothers with kindness, love and give respect to them we will surely clear our paths towards heaven. If we find our parents mother and father old and we take care of them then we gain rewards in this world and in life here after.

The Messenger of Allah (peace be upon him and his family) said:

"Every righteous child who casts a look of mercy and affection upon his parents shall be granted, for every look of his, rewards equivalent to that of an accepted Hajj."

Those around the Prophet questioned: "O' Prophet of Allah! Even if he were to look at them a hundred times a day?"

The Messenger of Allah (peace be upon him and his family) replied: "Indeed! Allah is the Greatest and Most Kind." (Biharul Anwar)

It is expected from a muslim to be kind and obedient towards his/her parents. Allah rewards each and every act of kindness in return. The Messenger of Allah (peace be upon him and his family) said:

> *"One, who follows the orders of Allah with regards to obeying parents, shall have two doors of Paradise opened up for him. And if there happens to be only one parent, one door of Paradise shall open up for him."*

Kanzul Ummal

36. STATUS OF MOTHER IS GREATER THAN FATHER

Once a man came to the Prophet (P.B.U.H) and said: "O Messenger of Allah! Who among the people is worthy of my good companionship?"

He replied: "Your mother."

The man again asked: "Then who?"

So he replied: "Your mother."

The man then asked one more time: "Then who?"

So the Prophet (P.B.U.H) replied again: "Your mother."

The man then asked: "Then who?"

So he replied: "Then your father." (Sahih Bukhari & Sahih Muslim).

The Prophet (P.B.U.H) repeated his answer "Your mother" three time to stress upon the status of mother and to tell his followers that status of mother is three degrees higher than a father.

37. MISBEHAVING WITH PARENTS IS NOT ALLOWED

Misbehaving with mother or father is not allowed by Islam in any case. Allah has told us in Holy Quran,

"Your Lord has decreed that you shall not worship anyone except Him, and [He has enjoined] kindness to parents. Should they reach old age at your side one of them or both do not say to them," Fie!" And do not scold them, but speak to them noble words. Lower the wing of humility to them, out of mercy, and say," My Lord!"

(Quran 17.23-24)

Islam has told us not to displease our mothers as mothers wrath will lead us to destruction. There is a story of the companion of Prophet (P.B.U.H) who fell

41

seriously ill and was approaching last moments of his life.

Prophet (P.B.U.H) asked him to utter these words, "Confess the uniqueness of Allah and say " There is no God but Allah'.""

The companion was unable to utter these words as his tongue was not supporting him in doing so. Prophet (P.B.U.H) then inquired about whether he has his mother alive or not. The lady in the room at that time told, " I am his mother".

The Prophet (P.B.U.H) asked her whether she is angry and dissatisfied with him, upon which she replied, " Yes! I have not been speaking with him for six years."

Prophet (P.B.U.H) requested her to forgive her son upon which she agreed. Then Prophet (P.B.U.H) again asked the companion, " Utter the same word now ' There is no God but Allah'." This time he easily uttered these words without any stammering.

38. REPAYMENT OF MOTHER'S SACRIFICE

In this life it is not possible for us to repay the favors that our mothers have given us no matter what we do for them. It is very important for Muslims to serve their parents in every possible way, the responsibility of parents is above any other responsibility in Islam. It is narrated that a companion of Prophet (P.B.U.H), Talhah ibn Muawiyah came to ask,

"I want to take part in a fight in the way of Allah."

He asked, "Is your mother alive?"

I replied, "Yes".

He then said, "Cling to her feet, as paradise is there." (Al Tabarani)

This tells us that serving one's mother has great reward.

Once Hazrat Abdullah Ibn Umar saw a Yemeni man performing Tawaf of Holy Ka'bah while carrying his mother on his back.

This man inquired Hazrat Umar, "I am like a tame camel to her! I have carried her more than she carried me. Do you think I have paid her back?"

Abdullah Ibn Umar replied ," No, not even one contraction!!" (Al-Adab al-Mufrad Bukhari)

39. WOMAN AS SISTERS.

After death of father all the responsibility of sisters lies on the shoulders of brothers until and unless they get married. Brothers must protect, support, and treat their sisters with kindness in the absence of their father. Sisters have the right of inheritance from their father's property and this right should be given to them without any hesitation.

40. DETAILS REGARDING RIGHT OF INHERITANCE.

In this book we have discussed several times about the right of inheritance that women has from the property of her ancestors. Islam gives the right of inheritance depending upon the responsibilities and relation that a person have with the deceased. It's not dependant upon whether the person is the first child or last child. The right of inheritance is dependant upon only two things:
1. Blood relation
2. Marriage.

41. RULE OF INHERITANCE FOR WIVES.

The first person in Quran who have the right of inheritance is wife. Wife gets one fourth of the share in case there are no children and one-eight if they have kids.

42. RULE OF INHERITANCE FOR DAUGHTERS

The second person to get the share of property is daughter. The share of daughter is different according to the number of brothers and sisters she has. Daughters are entitled to the share that is half of her brothers share that is brother gets 2/3rd while daughter get 1/3rd. In case there is only one daughter and no other siblings then she gets half of her father's property. If there are two or more daughters then they will get 2/3rd of the property which is equally divided.

In case there is a daughter , a wife and a father alive of the person who died then father will get 9/24th portion, wife gets 1/8th and daughter gets half of the property.

43. RIGHT OF A MOTHER IN INHERITANCE

In case the mother is still alive with one sibling of a person then it is commanded in Quran to give her the share of 1/3rd. If he has two or more siblings then her share will be 1/6th of the estate. The father is also entitled to one-sixth portion of the property in similar situations.

44. REASON OF DIFFERENCE IN PORTIONS AMONG MEN AND WOMEN

The question that arises here is why at some places the women gets the share that is less than the share of men in her family. The reason of doing so is quite clear. The share of property is divided first on the basis of how closely the person is related to the decedent, and then secondly it is based upon the responsibilities that every member carries upon him/her. In Islam the whole responsibility of running the matters of house i.e providing shelter, food, cloths and other necessities is upon the male member so that is the main reason of giving them the more share in some cases. While there are other cases in which the family structure is different and women gets more share as compared to men of the family due to nature of relation.

These are the few cases that I have discussed here regarding the law of inheritance. This law is quite detailed and is of great importance. Islam is a complete religion that emphasizes upon the protection of rights of every creature in this universe and that is the reason it has completely educated us regarding the law of inheritance. The main focus of this law is to protect the rights of every relation even after death of a person without any injustice.

45. WOMAN AND PREGNANCY.

Woman due to the hardships that she bears during pregnancy have higher status as a mother. In Islam there is a great reward for the period that a women spend in pregnancy.

At one place it is narrated by Imam as-Sadiq(as):

"Every time a woman becomes pregnant, during the whole period of pregnancy she has the status of one who fasts, one who worships during the night, and one who fights for Allah with her life and possessions. And when she is giving birth, Allah grants her so much reward that nobody knows its limit because of its greatness. And when she is giving milk to her child, for every suck of the child, Allah gives her the reward of freeing a slave from the children of Ismail, and when the period of breastfeeding the child is finished, one of the great angels of Allāh (SwT) taps her side and says: "Start your

47

> *deeds afresh, for Allah (SwT) has*
> *forgiven all your minor sins."*

If a woman dies while giving birth to a child then all her sins are forgiven due to the hardship and pain she had to face during that time as it is narrated from Imam as-Sadiq (as):

> *"Any time a woman leaves this*
> *world because of labour pains, on*
> *the Day of Judgement, Allah (SwT)*
> *will raise her from the grave pure*
> *and without an account (of sins),*
> *because such a woman has given*
> *her life due to the hardship and*
> *pain of labour ."*

Islam recommends to take special care of a woman who is about to give birth. It is recommended that she should stay happy and follow the Islamic practices more regularly as her good deeds will have an impact on the child who is going to get a new life.

Imam Ali (as) too, has said that in terms of Akhlaq, nature and religiousness, a child is made by the mother and obtains his/her disposition from her Akhlaq. Thus it is the responsibility of the mother that she creates the best possible environment for the first home of the child.

Pregnancy is a great gift of Allah for every woman and a start of a new phase of life so every woman should try to get the best out of it.

46. WOMAN AS A WARRIOR.

Muslim women are not less than anyone in this world. Whenever it is required by them to participate in economic activities they always do so successfully. History shows that many Muslim women participated actively during battles. Muslim women have also been a successful business runner, manager, rulers etc. So this is just the misconception regarding the women in Islam that they are suppressed and lesser than anyone.

From the times of Hazrat Muhammad (P.B.U.H) we find evidences that women at that time participated in the battles as the support for the fighters. Some women acted as nurse, some cooked food while some gave water to the soldiers.

Rufaida Al-Aslamia was the first muslim nurse who served the battlefield. She treated the wounds of Saad Ibn Muaath during the battle of Al-Khandaq. She was an expert in her field and transferred her knowledge to other women during that time. She led the group of volunteer nurses who provide treatments to the injured during battles and worked really well.

There is one more example of Umm Ammarah as a woman participating in the battle. Umm Ammarah participated in battle of Uhud with the purpose of providing water to the warriors. But due to certain reasons when she saw that it is required for her to participate in the battle in order to protect Hazrat Muhammad (P.B.U.H) she jumped in as a warrior and acted as a shield of Prophet Muhammad (P.B.U.H). That day Umm Ammarah received many wounds but she bravely fought. She also participated in the battle of Yamama where she lost her hand. It is narrated by Hazrat Umar (R.A) " On the day of 'Uhud, I heard the Messenger of Allah sallallahu 'alayhi wa sallam say, 'Whenever I looked to the right or left I saw her fighting in front of me'." Umm Ammarah was a brave women and has a respectful status in history of Islam.

47. POLITICAL AND SOCIAL SERVICES.

As we have already discussed that women have participated as nurses and carrier of water during battles. Muslim woman along with this social work have been very active in political activities as well. Woman have the full right to participate in government , public affairs, teaching and lawmaking thus every political and social activity.

48. MUSLIM WOMAN OF THE MODERN ERA.

The Muslim women of the modern era are not lagging behind women of any other society. They are competitive, passionate and committed towards success. Muslim women are fully equipped with the knowledge while staying within the limits that Islam teaches them. The concept of muslim woman as an illiterate is completely worthless. Islam promotes the seeking of knowledge for everyone regardless of man and woman. So how is it possible that women stay behind men in seeking of knowledge when it is recommended in Islamic teachings. Muslim women prefer education and they are actively participating in economic development along with men.

49. FAMILY COMES FIRST.

Muslim women according to the teachings of Islam prefer their home and family first as homemaking is the first responsibility that is on the shoulders of the women. But this does not mean that they can not take any other role in their life. There are many examples of women who excel in their professional life while maintaining the perfect balance between both job and family. But the reason for keeping the family as a first preference is required by nature, the responsibility of bringing a new life in this world and upbringing of kids is the job which is impossible for men to do even if they want to do so. That is why if we look at the muslim women in the history or in the modern era they always choose family over everything.

50. MISCONCEPTIONS ABOUT MUSLIM WOMAN

These days there are many misconceptions regarding the muslim women, most of the sources trying to spread these misconceptions are the ones who know least about Islam and rights of the people that Islam gives to everyone. Islam is the religion of peace, equality and justice.

The concept of muslim woman as the one who is suppressed and not allowed to do anything freely is totally wrong. The question here arises that how can a dress decide whether someone is independent or not? The woman of Islam chooses hijab over showing their body to the people who are stranger to her. Hijab gives women the right to freely go out and carryout her tasks without the fear of any unwanted interruption. Hijab stops females from provoking the opposite gender to harass them. Our clothes are meant to protect us, how can they hinder our progress?

Most of the time it is seen that domestic violence and not letting girls go out for education is associated with the muslim girls. So let me make this clear here that this has nothing to do with Islam, any kind of violence whether it is domestic or non-domestic is not at all allowed in Islam. The people who are true muslims do not believe in harming anyone whether men, women or children, they believe in love and peace in order to achieve higher place in the world hereafter.

As far as education is concerned we have discussed already in this book that how much importance Islam gives to the seeking of knowledge. Education and knowledge is not only important to excel in our professional careers but it also opens up our minds and let us respect each others right. Islam does not discriminate girl or a boy in any sense other than the responsibilities they have been assigned by the nature. Women have equal rights towards education, food, shelter and respect etc as much as men have. But there are some muslims who call themselves muslims but does not fully follow the practices of Islam and do injustice to women. Some of them are doing this because they are not ready to leave their traditions and culture that they think is everything to them.

Islam has its own culture which is based on simplicity, modesty, hospitality, respect and peace. Islam gives respect to men and women of all the religions. Islam does not allow Muslim to mistreat the women of different belief. Islam defines rights for the whole humanity which is not specific to any single religion. Allah and his last Prophet (P.B.U.H) has shown us the right path to lead this life, now it is upon us whether we choose that path or not, There are many muslims who by their clothes looks like true muslims but in reality they don't practice Islam properly. While on the other hand there are Muslims who does not follow the dress code strictly but are muslims truly by heart. Both to look like and to act like muslim is important. But to create a picture of Islam as a religion through the ones who does not practice it properly is wrong. It is important for us to understand the true teachings of Islam before judging everyone in the same manner.

Women in Islam has great respect whether she is a daughter, mother, sister, wife or any woman from the society. Hazrat Muhammad (P.B.U.H) has told us with his each and every action that how one should treat women. In Islamic history we find no evidence of domestic violence or injustice to the women. Even in the case of war or battle it is not allowed to harm women, children, elder or sick person,

Prophet Muhammad (P.B.U.H) said ,

"Do not kill any child, any woman, or any elder or sick person."

(Sunan Abu Dawud)

Islam indeed treats women like a queen, it has created rights for her that protects her from any sort of harsh realities of the societies. Men are given the task to protect them and provide for them. What other status could be the best for women? At most of the places the status of women in Islam is correctly stated in one golden sentence,

"When she is a daughter she opens door of Jannah for her father. When she is a wife she completes half of the deen of her husband. When she is a mother, Jannah lies under her feet- If everyone knew the true status of a muslim woman in Islam, even men would want to be woman."

(Quoted by Sheikh Akram Nadawi)

OTHER HELPFUL RESOURCES

- https://themuslimvibe.com/muslim-lifestyle-matters/parents/20-brilliant-hadiths-about-parents
- https://muflihun.com/abudawood/1/1
- https://sahih-bukhari.com/
- https://sunnah.com/muslim
- https://sunnah.com/tirmidhi
- https://sunnah.com/ibnmajah
- https://www.al-islam.org/status-mothers-islam-sayyid-muhammad-sohofi/status-mothers-islam

READ OTHER

50 THINGS TO KNOW

BOOKS

50 Things to Know

Website: 50thingstoknow.com

Facebook: facebook.com/50thingstoknow

Pinterest: pinterest.com/lbrennec

YouTube: youtube.com/user/50ThingsToKnow

Twitter: twitter.com/50ttk

Mailing List: Join the 50 Things to Know
Mailing List to Learn About New Releases

50 Things to Know

Please leave your honest review of this book on Amazon and Goodreads. We appreciate your positive and constructive feedback. Thank you.

Made in the USA
Las Vegas, NV
16 September 2023

77664030R00049